201
GREAT QUESTIONS

FOR MARRIED COUPLES

JERRY D. JONES

NavPress
BRINGING TRUTH TO LIFE
P.O. Box 35001, Colorado Springs, Colorado 80935

The Navigators is an international Christian organization. Our mission is to reach, disciple, and equip people to know Christ and to make Him known through successive generations. We envision multitudes of diverse people in the United States and every other nation who have a passionate love for Christ, live a lifestyle of sharing Christ's love, and multiply spiritual laborers among those without Christ.

NavPress is the publishing ministry of The Navigators. NavPress publications help believers learn biblical truth and apply what they learn to their lives and ministries. Our mission is to stimulate spiritual formation among our readers.

The people quoted in this book each have profound and thoughtful words worthy of our consideration. However, using their quotes for the purposes of this book in no way implies that we necessarily endorse or agree with all of their beliefs or values.

© 1999 by Jerry Jones
All rights reserved. No part of this publication may be reproduced in any form without written permission from NavPress, P.O. Box 35001, Colorado Springs, CO 80935
www.navpress.com
ISBN 1-57683-145-0

Printed in the United States of America

2 3 4 5 6 7 8 9 10 11 12 13 14 15 / 05 04 03 02

Contents

INTRODUCTION

The Power of the Question

For most of us who are in a relationship, at one time or another we have felt or said out loud, "Don't give me advice—just ask me questions and listen."

Author and theologian Sam Keen says that "nothing shapes our lives so much as the questions we ask." At the core of every life and story is a question, says author Gregg LeVoy. "We must come bearing questions. . . . Without [them] there is no discovery."

If we are going to continue learning about one another, it is necessary to continue asking questions—and then listen. Especially with those we think we know well.

Remember when you first met each other? How you were consumed to know more, to taste deeply of the mysteries, to understand all the wonderful aspects that make each of you unique and fascinating? You hungered for more. Far too often, in the routine of life, we neglect this marvelous discovery process with the "intimates" in our lives. We become tired. We lose the joy of wonder, of mystery. And that is our loss.

That's what this book is designed for: to help you reconnect with the qualities of your partner that you hold most dear. This is not a book of answers. Rather, it is a toolbox full of ready-to-use questions to help renew the discovery experience, to give it new legs within the context and safety of the one person you have chosen as your life partner. Use this book to help you get out of the rut and give your relationship new shape and meaning. Use it to help you not (in the words of John Michael Talbot) be "preoccupied with the superficial at the expense of the meaningful." Allow this little book to take you to a deeper place—together.

A Few Suggested Goals and Guidelines

1

These questions are designed to help you celebrate each other, to listen, to learn, to dream, to remind you of why God brought you together, what holds you together, and what makes you unique. Use this book

- in conversations around the dinner table
- on your "date night"
- while traveling in the car (keep a copy in your glove box)
- over a Saturday morning cup of coffee
- on a weekend getaway
- before shared Bible reading and prayer
- at bedtime

2

Some questions are intended to be serious, some more playful and humorous. But all are intended to help you discover a little more about the mystery of the multifaceted person you are spending your life with. Remember that in most cases these are not intended to be questions requiring right or wrong answers. The purpose is not to get a good grade but to learn about the feelings, thoughts, and values of each other. Use this as a tool to help improve or enhance your conversations and mutual discovery times together. The more honest and authentic you can be when answering, the better will be the results—and the more effective these times of conversation will be.

3

Keep in mind that often just one question, along with other thoughts or feelings it may bring to mind, can require quality time. That's okay. It is better to go slowly and gain deeper understanding—plus have fun in the process—than to race through this book. View this small, handy resource as a longtime companion that you can go back to again and again.

4

The questions are not designed to be a way to pry into especially difficult areas where your mate may be uncomfortable to go. Nor is the information revealed during these sharing times meant to be used against your partner later. Treat this sharing and discovery process as confidential and sacred.

5

There is no need to be frightened on this marvelous discovery journey. You will note that the book begins with easier, less vulnerable questions and progresses to deeper, more thoughtful topics. Go at your own pace. But feel free to break the rules if your both are so inclined. This is one book you are not required to read from front to back. You also have permission to use "I" instead of "you" where applicable or to rephrase the questions to make them more personal.

6

And finally, remember that even God—who already knew all the answers—found it useful to ask questions of people in the Bible at leas forty-five times. Invite Him to be with you in this love-renewing growth and discovery process.

HOW TO USE THIS BOOK IN GROUPS

While the questions in this book are designed to be used by a couple alone together, many can be adapted for use in a group. For example, a couples small-group Bible study might want to use one or two of these questions as openers at the beginning of their time together each week (although you may want to think twice before using some of the more intimate, probing questions in a public setting).

If you use the questions in a group, you will need to rephrase some of them. In most cases it's just a matter of changing pronouns around.

Instead of:
If you were to compare our marriage to a particular sport, which sport would you choose, and why?

Ask:
If you were to compare your marriage to a particular sport, which sport would you choose, and why?

There's plenty of room on each page to pencil in your rewording ahead of time, if you wish.

Whether couples use this book in their private times together or in groups of married persons, my prayer is that it may begin many warm, invigorating conversations that strengthen many marriages.

1

If I had a perfectly identical twin, what questions would you ask to tell us apart? Is there anything you could say that would make me—but not my sibling—burst out laughing?

2

Among our new acquaintances, who would you like us to do something with socially? Why? What would you like us to do with this person (or persons)?

<u>3</u>

If we could relive our dating period, what would you like us to do differently? What would you like us to do the same? Why?

4

Is romantic love a necessity or a luxury in today's world? Explain your choice. How might it have been different in the time of our great-grandparents?

5

For you, is our marriage more like a river or an ocean? In what ways?

6

Researchers have found that people have a greater tendency to fall in love when they are experiencing danger.* How has danger played a part in our relationship in the past? How might danger enhance our feelings of passion and love in the present?

*You may also think in terms of a shared challenge or hardship.

7

What is the most romantic thing
you've ever done with me
or for me?

8

If you were an advertiser trying to
catch my attention in less than a
minute, what would you do?

9

What is the first clue that
indicates I am flirting with you?
Do you wish there were more
flirting in our marriage?
If so, in what ways?

10

Of all our single friends,
which two do you think would
make the best match? Why?

11

Imagine that our romance is going to be turned into a movie. What will provide the high points of the drama?

12

If we were to play a game of show-and-tell about our marriage, what object would you pick to tell about, and why?

13

If we were to go on a shopping spree together—to buy something special just for the two of us—what would we most likely come home with?

14

What are five things you remember about when we first met? About our first date? About our first kiss? About the first time I met your parents?

15

If I were to kidnap you and take you someplace exotic, where would you like that place to be? What would you most resist about this kidnapping? What would you most like about it?

16

When do you find me most
irresistibly attractive?

17

When you describe me to someone who has never met me, which physical features of mine do you mention first? Which character qualities do you mention first?

18

In what ways have I been your teacher? What grades do you expect to receive from me? What grades do you deserve?

19

If we could both run away and join the circus, what jobs would we want to get? What would you most enjoy about the experience?

20

What do you imagine it is about me that causes angels to dance?

21

When did you first realize that
you were in love with me?
Describe the setting and how
you knew.

22

How is marriage like walking
along the edge of a cliff
blindfolded?

23

We've all heard the phrase "Diamonds are forever." Other than diamonds, what gift best represents forever to you?

24

In what ways has our marriage helped you believe in miracles?

25

What was your all-time favorite "date night" we've had since we've been married? What made it so memorable?

26

If you were to compare our marriage to a particular sport, which sport would you choose, and why?

27

What are some college courses or adult education classes that sound inviting to you? Which of these, if any, do you think we would enjoy taking together?

28

Assume for a moment that we are not married. How would you describe yourself in a personal ad in the newspaper? How would you describe me?

29

What is something silly we did together that you vividly recall? Do you think we should be more spontaneous and playful?

30

For a moment, think of our marriage as a swimming pool. Are you on the diving board or in the water? In what ways?

31

Do you enjoy listening to me read to you? Why or why not? If you do enjoy it, when would you like me to read to you more?

32

For you, what was the most memorable vacation we've taken together since our marriage? If we could go anywhere on a vacation, where would you like us to go?

33

When I am not around, how are you most likely to brag about me to others?

34

Other than the bedroom, what room in our house is your favorite place to spend time with me? Why?

35

What are three things you like about me (and would like even if we were not married)?

36

What are five of the little, seemingly insignificant things in our marriage that mean the most to you?

37

If you knew that all photos of me were going to be destroyed and you could rescue only one of them, which one would it be? Why?

38

What are three ways that you are most fulfilled by me?

39

What do you find most attractive about me? Has what you find attractive in me changed in any way from when we were dating?

40

If you were to come up with a new pet name for me—one to be used only when we're alone together—what would it be?

41

At the heart of many of the world's great love stories is an obstacle — something that threatens to keep the lovers apart. What have been our obstacles? Have they increased or decreased our passion for one another?

42

In what ways do you feel
nurtured in our marriage?

43

Excluding touch, what is it about
me that brings you the
most pleasure?

44

If I were to set aside one month as a special time for romancing you, what are at least four things you would want me to do during the month?

45

In your opinion, what is the greatest myth about love? What is the greatest myth about marriage?

46

What is something you'd like to see me do that would be totally out of character for me? Why would you choose that?

47

What are at least three reasons why you chose to marry me? What are three reasons why you would choose to marry me all over again?

48

If you had to travel overseas for a long period of time, what would you take to remind you of me and of our life together?

49

Researchers believe that a primary cause of stress is things left incomplete in a person's life—the more things left incomplete, the more stress. What are the "incompletes" in our life together that are causing you stress?

50

Rene Yasenek once said, "Kissing is a means of getting two people so close together that they can't see anything wrong with each other." When are you least aware of my imperfections?

What is something you look forward to in our relationship during this coming year? In the next ten years?

52

What is one of the best conversations you can remember us having? What made it so memorable? What are several topics you would like us to spend more time talking about?

53

In what ways am I most likely to keep you guessing?

54

Mark Twain once said, "Twenty years from now you will be more disappointed by the things you didn't do than by the ones you did do. So throw off the bowlines. Sail away from the safe harbor. . . . Explore. Dream. Discover." Twenty years from now, what will you be most disappointed about not having done—if you do not do it? In what ways do I encourage or discourage you from pursuing your dreams?

55

If you knew for certain that neither of us would ever die — that we would live forever on this earth and not grow old — what would you like us to do differently in our marriage? Would our love and passion tend to be stronger or weaker? Why?

56

What is it that you tend to have the most fears about? How do you express your fears, and how is that different from how I express mine?

57

Do you think that being happily married and committed to one's mate will be more of a status symbol twenty-five years from now than it is today? What would have to change to bring that about?

58

Mignon McLaughlin once said, "A successful marriage is one in which you fall in love many times, always with the same person." In what ways have you found yourself falling in love with me more than once?

59

In what ways do you have the greatest confidence in my intentions?

60

Where do we need more originality in our marriage? In what ways could this add sparkle and jazz?

61

Is it possible to have love without happiness? Why or why not?

62

Robert Frost once said, "Love is an irresistible desire to be irresistibly desired." Describe what being irresistibly desired looks like to you.

63

If your life were a sermon, what would be the message? If it had the customary three points, what would they be?

64

In what ways do I have a better opinion of you than you think you deserve? In what ways do I have a worse opinion of you than you deserve?

65

If you were to write one golden rule for a happy, healthy marriage, what would this rule be?

66

In what ways are we a perfect match? In what ways do our differences create friction? What can we do to capitalize on our differences so they enhance our marriage?

67

André Maurois once said, "Marriage is an edifice that must be rebuilt every day." What are some things I could do to help in this daily rebuilding?

68

From living with me on a daily basis, what have you learned about the character and attributes of God?

69

What do you find more attractive in me: my strength or my vulnerability? What do you value in each of these qualities?

70

In our marriage, do you feel more like a sailor on the sea or a gardener in a garden? Why?

71

G. K. Chesterton once said,
"Marriage is an armed alliance
against the world." In what ways
are we like armed allies?

72

In what ways do I inspire you?

73

Some marriages are built around maintaining peace while others are committed to nurturing love. Does our relationship favor peace or love? What steps could we take to improve both?

74

In what ways could I better encourage you to nurture your soul—to have quality times of personal contemplation, reflection, and prayer?

75

What qualities of mine would you like our children to inherit from me? Or what qualities of mine would you like to have?

76

Charles Handy once said, "It is one of the paradoxes of success that the things and ways which got you there are seldom those things that keep you there." What are the "things and ways" in our marriage that got us to this point but that will not keep us here?

77

Does our marriage need more or less silence? In what ways?

78

In what ways is our marriage a pleasurable aroma to God?

79

When do you feel most blessed to have me as your mate?

80

In what ways is our marriage awkward for you? In what ways is it natural?

81

Imagine that ours is a Jewish family living in central Europe during the Nazi era. Knowing what you now know about the Holocaust, what methods would you use to prevent being separated from me and our children? What would you be willing to sacrifice for us to stay together and remain safe?

82

How has our marriage helped you fulfill one or more of your most cherished desires? What is at least one desire that you have yet to fulfill?

83

Is agreement always necessary for harmony? Why or why not?

84

ʾWhat in our relationship makes you feel refreshed? Guilty? Exhilarated? Mischievous? Worried?

85

Someone once said,
"In the majority of couples, love
consists of one party loving and
the other allowing himself to be
loved." Is that true in our
marriage? If so, which of us is
more likely to be the one loving,
and which is the one allowing
himself or herself to be loved?
Why?

86

In what ways does our marriage remind you of a dormant volcano, if at all?

87

In what ways do you need to be needed by me? In what ways might you confuse love with need?

88

Some people believe that in order to grow, learn, and stay on the cutting edge, we must occasionally do something that makes us feel insecure. What is something you have done on purpose, fully knowing that it would make you feel insecure? Do I help you at such times, or hinder you?

89

What other couple's marriage do you most admire? Why? What is it about their relationship you wish we had more of in ours?

90

When do you feel most lonely?

91

Where are you most tempted to want to change me? Why? How does this impact our relationship?

92

What are at least three things that have a potential to become a wedge between us? In what ways can we protect our marriage from these wedges?

93

Where are you currently most satisfied in our marriage? Where are you most dissatisfied?

94

In what ways has our marriage added to those things that you like about yourself?

95

When do you feel most supported
by me? When do you feel most
respected by me?

96

Tell about one of the most fun
times we've ever had working
together around the house.

97

What is it I do that encourages the little child in you to come out and play? What do you most like about the little child in me?

98

In what ways do you wish I were more aggressive or more passive? Why?

99

Susan B. Anthony once said, "In life, actions speak louder than words, but in love, the eyes do." In what ways do my eyes speak to you? What do you find most intriguing about my eyes?

100

When do you feel most listened to by me? Describe a recent time when you felt this. When do you feel least listened to by me?

101

In what ways do we deserve an award for mutual submission?

102

In what ways are you comfortable with our showing affection to one another in public? In what ways are you uncomfortable with that?

103

If I were to give you something out of the ordinary for each day this next week—something that did not require money but required my time and energy—what seven gifts would you most like to receive from me?

104

What is something about me or our life together that you feel thankful for—but seldom express your thanks for?

105

What is it about me that helps you trust God more?

106

Are there times when you wish I would touch you more? What are those cues signaling your need to be touched that I'm not picking up on?

107

What are three things that help
you feel closely connected to me?

108

What is one thing you love doing
that you wish I loved more?

109

Someone once said, "The easiest thing about love is kissing and holding hands." Do you agree or disagree? What is the hardest thing about love?

110

What is the most subtle yet sensual thing I do to you?

111

If we were to write a one-sentence purpose statement for our marriage, what would it be?

112

In what ways am I helping you to be better prepared for the world to come?

113

Of all the gifts I have ever given you, which is your favorite? What is so special to you about this gift?

114

In our marriage, are you more likely to have medals or scars? Why?

115

Democritus of Abdera once said, "The life without festival is a long road without an inn." In our marriage, where do we need more festival and less road?

116

If we could repeat one of our romantic experiences, which would you choose? In what ways do you wish I were more romantic?

117

What do you wish we had more of in our marriage: romance or friendship? Why?

118

When do you feel most cherished by me? When is it that you most cherish me?

119

Describe one of the funnier memories you have of me. How might there be more laughter in our marriage?

120

What are some important lessons about intimacy that you've learned from me?

121

What is a personal accomplishment of mine that has made you proud? Why is that?

122

What are your favorite nonverbal signals that we sometimes use to communicate privately with one another when others are present?

123

What is your most creative,
imaginative idea for a love note
you would like to receive
from me?

124

If you were to give me a trophy, what would it be for? What would this trophy look like and be made of? Where would you like to see it displayed?

125

When you make a mistake, what is it I do (or don't do) that you most appreciate? Why?

126

What do you wish you had realized sooner about marriage?

127

If we had a "memory chest" for our years together, what are ten things you would want to put in it?

128

What is your favorite way to spend those moments when there are no interruptions, no appointments, no noises? If we knew we were going to have such an afternoon together, how would you plan to spend it?

129

What is the most extravagant thing I've ever done to express my love for you? If money were no object, what is something you would like me to do?

130

In what ways am I your biggest cheerleader? In what ways do you need more cheerleading from me?

131

What are the conflicts in our marriage that help kindle healthy passion in our relationship?

132

Are you more likely to believe that the future is too terrifying to think about or that the past is too painful to remember? Why? How can I help you with your fear or pain?

133

What three compliments do you most enjoy getting from me? What is it I do that makes you feel most flattered?

134

Do I fight fair? Why or why not? In what ways would you like to see our "fighting rules" changed?

135

What imperfections in me no longer bother you as they once did?

136

What is the riskiest thing I have ever done with you? In what ways can being risky enhance or harm our marriage?

137

If our marriage were a business, how would you describe our commitment to quality? Where do we most need to improve the quality? Why?

138

How do we establish priorities for our marriage? What are your top five priorities for us?

139

Describe a time when I did something that surprised you in a pleasant way. What was it you most enjoyed about this surprise?

140

In what ways do you consider me
wise? What is the best advice
I have ever given you? Under
what circumstances do you wish
I would ask for your advice
more often?

141

If you had to come up with a metaphor to describe your life, what would it be? What metaphor would best describe our marriage?

142

Describe a time when we explored something together. What did you enjoy about this exploration? What is something you'd still like to explore with me?

143

Ecclesiastes 4:9-12 says, "Two people can accomplish more than twice as much as one. . . . If one person falls, the other can reach out and help. . . . A person standing alone can be attacked and defeated, but two can stand back-to-back and conquer" (NLT). How has this been true in our marriage?

144

What three traditions or customs do we have in our marriage that you most value? Why? What is one tradition you would like us to establish?

145

In what ways do you wish you had more feedback from me?

146

Think back to our dating experiences before our marriage. What things did we do then that you miss and want to do again?

147

In what ways do you most see sacrificial love from me?

148

What are three things you need to hear me express more often?

149

If I were to die today, what would be three of your most cherished memories of me? What specific tastes, smells, sounds, or sights would bring me to your mind? What would be your biggest regret?

150

Sleeping Beauty waited one hundred years for the handsome prince to awaken her from a trance. What is one thing you are waiting for in our marriage?

151

King Solomon once wrote, "You are stately as a palm tree, and your breasts are like its clusters. I say I will climb the palm tree and lay hold of its branches. Oh, may your breasts be like clusters of the vine, and the scent of your breath like apples" (Song of Songs 7:7-8, NRSV). If I were to write something similar to you—in my own words—how would you feel about it? Why?

152

What is the greatest rival you have to fend off to attain the kind of loving relationship with me you desire?

153

Is there anything about me that I don't like but you do?

154

Three common myths are that money will make us secure, power will make us important, and fame will make us happy. Which of these three myths are you and I most likely to believe? Why?

155

In 1 Corinthians 13, Paul tells us there are nine components to love: patience, kindness, generosity, humility, courtesy, unselfishness, good temper, trust, and sincerity. Which of these components am I most likely to live out in our marriage? Which of these components am I least likely to live out?

156

What are your expectations about a marriage partner that I am not fulfilling? In what ways are these expectations realistic or unrealistic? How essential are they to having a happy, fulfilling marriage?

157

What are five things you believe absolutely (with no doubts) about our marriage relationship?

158

What do you most want right now in our marriage? What three areas of your life need the most attention from me right now?

159

We've all heard the story of the frog who turned into a handsome prince after being kissed by the princess. In what ways have I helped turn you into someone more desirable? In what ways have you done the same for me?

160

What is it we say or do to one another in public that makes onlookers think less of us? What do we say or do that makes them think more of us?

161

In what ways have you traded ambition for love? In what ways have you traded love for ambition?

162

E. Stanley Jones once said, "O Christ, do not give me tasks equal to my powers, but give me powers equal to my tasks, for I want to be stretched by things too great for me." Where do you want to be stretched for greatness in your personal life? In our marriage?

163

Someone once said, "It is when we earn love least that we need it most." In what ways have you experienced this in our marriage?

164

Where are you most inhibited in our relationship? Why? What could help you lose some of your inhibitions?

165

When do you feel that you are missing something important in our life together?

166

What room in my life do you have the hardest time getting into? Why is that?

167

If you were forced to give up all control in our marriage, what would be the hardest area of control for you to let go of? Why?

168

If you knew you were going to die tomorrow, what would matter less to you about our marriage, and what would matter more?

169

In our marriage, are you more often the authority or the rebel against authority? Why? What does this add or subtract to our marriage?

170

In what ways do we keep score?

171

Someone once said, "Success is getting what you want; happiness is wanting what you get." Are you more likely to consider yourself happy or successful? Why?

172

Author Leo Tolstoy gave his diary to his fiancée so that he would have no secrets from her. What would have happened if we had known everything about each other before our marriage? Is there ever a time now, as a married couple, that we should keep secrets from each other?

173

What three relational goals would you like us to accomplish in our marriage during the next twelve months?

174

At the core of who I am, what do you find most noble and decent in me?

175

What are three of your buried dreams? What are three of your secret doubts?

176

In what ways have you been broken or wounded by love? What have been the consequences of that for our marriage?

177

What do you have the hardest time asking me for (or about) sexually? Why is this difficult or uncomfortable for you?

178

What in our marriage must be torn down before we can build something new in its place?

179

When is physical affection most satisfying for you? When is it least welcome?

180

What are three examples of how I have gained your trust?

181

When we argue, do you usually think I am more interested in winning or in understanding? What do I do that makes you think this?

182

What are three important decisions affecting our marriage that we have been putting off? Why have we done that?

183

Describe what you consider to be the "open doors" and the "closed doors" in our marriage. In what ways, if any, would you like to see these situations change?

184

What are at least three secrets we share that no one else knows? How does our sharing secrets make you feel?

185

If we were Adam and Eve, what would be our forbidden fruit?

186

What do you most like about hearing me pray? What do my prayers tell you about who God is in my life?

187

In what ways do you wish you had more courage? What would you have done differently in life thus far if you had had more courage? How can I help you become more courageous?

188

What three things about our marriage will never change regardless of the circumstances?

189

When do you have the hardest time saying, "I love you"? When do you have the hardest time saying, "I'm sorry"?

190

What have we done in our marriage that began as something undesirable—something we did not look forward to doing—but that had a positive, pleasant result?

191

Robert Quillen once said,
"A happy marriage is the union of
two good forgivers." What do you
see as our strengths and
weaknesses as forgivers?

192

What are the words you most
regret saying to me? What are the
words you most value hearing
from me? Why?

193

What remains your deepest
unsolved mystery about me?
Does this mystery enchant,
frustrate, or scare you? Why?

194

When are you most likely to be
jealous of me?

195

What are three things that sound like fun but you think you'd probably never do? How can I help you overcome your reluctance?

196

When do you feel unjustly blamed by me?

197

George Bernard Shaw once said, "There are two sources of unhappiness in life. One is not getting what you want; the other is getting it." From which of these sources do you get more of your unhappiness? How do I fit into this?

198

In what ways does your happiness depend on changes I need to make?

199

Do you ever feel that no matter what you do in our marriage, it is never good enough for you? For me? If so, explain why you feel that way.

200

What three questions (not included in this book) do you wish that I would ask you?

201

What feelings seem most risky for you to share with me? When do you feel most vulnerable with me?

Author

JERRY JONES is a free-lance writer working on his first historical novel. Over the past twenty years he has helped edit, write, or develop more than twenty-five books, served as editor of three national periodicals, and helped launch a national ministry. He values time with both his immediate and extended family and loves serving as the editor of a biannual family newsletter. Jerry lives in a creekside cottage in the mountains near Colorado Springs, Colorado.

IMPROVE YOUR SMALL GROUP AND PERSONAL RELATIONSHIPS.

201 Great Questions

Ideal for getting conversations started in small groups or for hanging out with friends, this book gives you the opportunity to learn more about others--and about yourself.

201 Great Questions
(Jerry D. Jones) $6

201 Great Questions to Help Simplify Your Life

Evaluate those difficult-to-balance tasks and obligations to bring into focus the things that really matter. Re-direct your life into simpler patterns that affect your thinking and daily habits. Useful for both individual and group reflections.

201 Great Questions to Help Simplify Your Life
(Jerry D. Jones) $6

201 Great Questions for Parents and Children

This easy-to-use tool helps parents interact with their children to build mutual understanding and deeper family relationships as they discuss their perspectives and problems.

201 Great Questions for Parents and Children
(Jerry D. Jones) $6

Get your copies today at your local bookstore, visit our website at www.navpress.com, or call (800) 366-7788 and ask for offer #**2300** or a FREE catalog of NavPress products

NAVPRESS
BRINGING TRUTH TO LIFE
www.navpress.com
Prices subject to change.